Waterfall of Intentions
Poetry Collection

THERESA JONES

First Published in 2022

by AboutTime4T Publishing

Copyright & Related Rights Act 2000.

Photograhic Images by: Pat Burns (patburns59@icloud.com)

Paperback ISBN: 978-1-8382943-2-8

Acknowledgements

I am very lucky to belong to local writing groups with a fabulous group of talented writers who support, inspire and motivate the writer within.

Huge thanks for the fabulous support needed for this book:
Eileen Acheson, a wonderful poet and friend, who gave endless advice. Eileen is the author of the wonderful poetry collection - "*I Wonder*", founder of 'tellyourstorywitheileen.ie'

Pat Burns, photographer based in Co. Meath; for the breathtaking photographs.
Boyne River (Cover), White Rose, images from Laytown Beach, Two Trees and The Mountain path.
Author of photographic collection and memories
"Laytown, through the years".

I was very lucky to meet Ella Doolan through her Work Experience project. Ella is an animation student at the Technological University of the Shannon (TUS) – (Marie Walsh). This project was a collaboration between TUS, Writing Change Lives (Margaret O'Brien) and managed by the Tudor Artisan Hub in Carrick-on-Suir, (Linda Fahy). I hope you agree, her work is fabulous!

Ella Doolan (@ellas_doodles, illustrator, whose beautiful illustrations for my shorter poems breathed life to reveal the whole meaning of the words in
Servant of Time,
Mask, Bitterness, Risen Shards, Observers and section images for Observations and Memories.

About this book

Waterfall of Intentions is a collection of narrative poetry
where I try to tell a story in a few verses.
The poems hold a mirror to yourself to realize
that you cannot be all things to all people.

This narrative poetry collection is told in four sections:

Reflections on Life & Nature

Relationships

Observations

Memories

Kind Words for Servant of Time

Servant of Time was my first poetry collection written to reflect a time of chaos and challenges, in this collection, I was able to slay my dragons and allow them to rest on the page. Here are some kind words for this collection:

'Theresa Jones has a refined sense of and appreciation for the people, places and events that have influenced her. She returns to them with a keen and felt recall, finding poetry on an early morning milk float in her native London and in the many areas of natural beauty in her adopted Clonmel.'
Margaret Galvin Writer and Editor

'This collection of poems, by Theresa Jones, will inspire you with honesty and resilience. Theresa's sense of irony hits top notes that will resonate and reverberate. Her unmistakeable voice and it's love of nature and people make this collection, like herself, a unique gift to be treasured.'
Eileen Acheson, Writer

v

Servant of Time
*for my brother Maurice, who gifted me
some of the words that came to him in a dream.*

The cloak of the Reaper brushes the earth.
Death is a stowaway,
it goes away
but comes back another day.

Collecting souls.
Harvesting some,
rejecting others
whose hourglass holds sand still to be used.

A subtle rebuke for a gift not valued,
while many worthy of life battle
to hold on to the mortal coil.
Claimed too early,
subject to the Grim Reaper's scythe.

He is not judge or jury
but a farmer reaping his crop.
Souls released from one life
to await rebirth in another.

Not judge nor jury.
He is not to blame.
Just a servant of time
when the hourglass is empty.

(taken from my first poetry collection, Servant of Time)

vii

Kind Words for Waterfall of Intentions

'Theresa is a poet and a person with a clear eye.
She takes the reader on a journey to forest, mountain and sea;
into the inner heartland. You will experience a truly unique voice
in the company of Waterfall of Intentions.
Enjoy.'

**Eileen Acheson - Writer,
author of "I Wonder, Poetry Collection"**

Dedications

For my lovely children,
Jenny and Michael

Table of Contents

Morning Moon

**Dipped between
the hills,
the full moon
kisses the earth
good day.**

Reflections on Life & Nature

Allow nature to restore
your sanity, your peace.
Bring balance to your world.

Waterfall of Intentions

I set my stone at the waterfall of intentions.
My poor man's diamond, the quartz
sparkles in the forest light.

I ask for patience, peace and courage
in this blissful green oasis
of lichen, moss and fern.

Clear stream waters carry away
my fears and anxieties.
My soul is soothed by
this tranquil cathedral of nature.

Chase Your Rainbow

There are days when you are asked to
move that moon a little to the left,
to make room for the sun,
don't obscure the light.

Constant demands,
push those goalposts a little farther.
More, more, more.
Somehow wrong, could always do a little better.

Strive toward the undefined, unobtainable.
Challenge after challenge.
No goal, no measure.
Unattainable trophy.

To those who can move the sun and moon.
Create a new universe, reach for the stars.
Dance through life's showers.
Just chase your rainbow

A Simple Thank You

Do you wonder why
Thank you
is the hardest word for some people?

To award credit for value added,
improvements made.
Help or support freely given to another.

A simple thank you
costs
nothing.

Kindness
returns
kindness.

What is the cost
to the self-worth
to value that of another.

The receiver need only
make a show of appreciation,
token words spoken with a smile.

Unwelcome Guest

Garden feeders full, seed scattered,
begin the ballet of feathers,
dine together,
establish a pecking order.

A drama unfolds between
a gutsy robin and a young crow.
A turf cold war.

The crow watches carefully,
tilts its head to cast a guilty eye in my direction
taught by its elders
that it may be an unwelcome guest
not invited to dine.

Robin has no such worries,
secure in his place, darts in,
robs the seed from under crow's beak.
Clearly fortune favours the bold.

Imprint
for Michael

Crash against the window.
Brown, black, grey speckled wings beat fast
to match the blood pumping
to the young hawk's heart.

Rescued from the ledge,
talons grip the knuckle tight.
Balance instills confidence,
velvet smooth wings settle into a calm pose.

An imprint made between human and hawk.
Talons wrapped around the soul.
A life connection forged.

Messages in Dreams

There is a message in my dreams,
if only
I could understand them.

My childhood home haunts my nights.
I wander for hours
trapped in a maze of rooms in
a house lost to me.

I am accompanied by family
who passed on many years ago.
I realise that the messages will be repeated
until I understand their meaning.

I hold these loved ones with me,
but they need to be released.
I must sanction their onward journey
It is time for me to travel on alone.

Nights for the Fire

Enjoy the end of Summer.
Time to prepare,
Winter is approaching.

Robin song, dying Summer breeze.
Nature whispers in deeper tones
that Autumn has begun its journey.
Migrating birds herald a time of slowing down.

Almost welcome after long Summer evenings.
Endless chores grass growing, grass mowing.
Complete outside jobs, so much to do.

Walk a little further while the evening is fair.
While there is a stretch make sure to stretch your legs.
Dress for sharp breeze or soft rain.

For evenings will draw in.
Enjoy the last long days before
there are only nights for the fire.

Waiting on the Strand

Grey pebbles roll in and out on a receding tide.
Grey sky meets shoreline on Woodstown Strand.
The long draw of waves across the stones,
short sigh as the waves are drawn back.

Slow breathe in, HOLD, slow breathe out.
Match the rhythm of nature until calm.
Watch the waves, lost in today.
Grey pebbles roll in and out on a receding tide.

Further down the beach,
black Labrador zig zags drawn to driftwood, glances back.
Races to a red jacket zipped to the neck.
Blue woolly hat, head down against the biting wind.
Blue fingers hold a dangling lead.

Grey pebbles roll in and out on a receding tide.
Slow breathe in. HOLD. Slow breathe out.
Hoarse cry of seagulls on the wind.
Resting seabirds bob on the waves.

Remain still to catch mobile phone signal.
Wait to hear the words - return for tests or go home, all clear.
Scan the copper coast, light grey clouds hover.
Mobile vibrates. Go home.

Slow breathe in.
HOLD.
Slow breathe out.
Grey pebbles roll in and out on a receding tide
on Woodstown Strand.

25

The Foundations of Life

Gardening is my sanctuary, restores order from chaos.
My father taught me to prune roses; a third in March,
two thirds in October.
Before a frost, double dig for weeds,
leave roots exposed to minimise your work.
Before seeds; dig, hoe, work soil till fine. Preparation is the key.

My Mother taught me the rule of three,
take three cuttings with one for luck.
Make sure there is a bit of old and a bit of new.
Strip the stalk, plant to the first node where the roots will grow.
Natures rules, rituals observed for success.

On life, my father said, "Spend some,
save some to keep for a rainy day",
then it will be there when needed.
Always remember good manners, "Manners maketh the man".
or when dithering on a decision, "if in doubt, do nought".

My Mother said every weekend,
"a little bit of what you fancy does you good".
When disappointment struck, "If it's meant to be, it will happen.
It will all be alright in the end".
Of things just a little broken,
"keep it, put it in the shed, it may come in useful".

Two decades of rituals and sayings,
laid the foundations of my life.
Although three decades gone, my parents are with me every day.
Words and rituals passed on to my own children,
who in time may do the same.

The Copper Beech & The Ivy

The copper beech stood tall, vibrant.
Crowned in leaves of deep purple,
dark blood red, majestic, glorious.

Young ivy clung to the trunk,
tendrils groping at the bark,
seeking a route to the light.

Copper beech lent support.
The ivy and beech entwined, in the sunshine.
Glossy green smothered deep red.

Beech began to bend
under the weight of the vine.
Branches confined, wrapped tight, it craved release.

Ivy chose not to understand,
its own need
too great.

Beech, an unwilling host to an ungrateful guest.
Destined to be a wooden cane
to bear the weight of another, withered and died.

Stone of Affirmation

Today marks a new start.

A small white sparkling quartz stone
has been set at the Waterfall of Intentions,
the last in a rock pile now obscuring the pool.

Many troubles and affirmations for years.
Rocks, stones, pebbles, more rocks.
A pile of sorrows,
this waterfall has carried away.

A stone of affirmation is set in a new pile.
Black quartz for a new start,
the intense dark glossy velvet of the rock
sucks in the gaze, focuses the mind.

Silence,
while the words are spoken to the wind.
It is now time for the waterfall
to carry future affirmations of hope.

Hope
that life will improve.

Happiness
that today is good.

Confidence
that you are strong enough.

Relationships

Couples can be physically close
but remain
emotionally distant.

How easy to judge
another through the lens
of our own reality.

The Romance Season

February, the month of romance.
Short days, dark nights, isolation,
the melancholy month.

Remember,
it is better to be safe in a tiny house alone
than fearful in a large house in company.

It is better
to be on the shelf
than in the wrong cupboard.

It is better
to be comfortable in your own skin
whatever its size
than striving for undefined perfection.

On the Menu

If a table has been laid
with a banquet of mistakes,
even a good man will feast upon them.

To learn your lessons of the past,
Check the menu for your errors before
you allow another to dine at your expense.

Lessons Learnt

Set your boundaries before you leave the house,
tell a someone your dog is alone and where your keys are,
unless they are the same person.
Enjoy your day.

The guide to walking a new route, new relationship, new friendship.

These are the lessons learned from one to six.

One – drop a map pin on your phone so you know where you parked *(imagination – so the police can find the body)* (reality) you can find your way back to your car.

Two – check the area for a map of the walk or arrows for guidance. Don't ask another walker, they may not know but be quick to send you in the wrong direction.

Three – Bring money, tissues, charged phone with location on, and a mask for COVID. You may need a cup of tea.

Four – Be careful to keep your conversations from deep personal topics. Don't light conversational beacons on mistakes of the past. Dodge those questions, don't lay breadcrumbs for someone to follow.

Five – go back to four and read again. Don't guide someone in to take advantage of your weaknesses or as its now called "healing work in progress". Your good nature will be exploited.

Six – If you overshare, you have provided the key to unlock your mind and steal your peace.

35

Phases

Full moon ritual of release; a time of personal reflection.

Excitement – anticipation of meeting someone new.

My mind throws up barricades, endless conversation, chatter, a stream of words, a flow to provoke a response in the listener. A veil to observe them behind. Responses are gauged for being on topic, following subject changes, analyse for engagement of minds. Nuances evaluated for annoyance, disagreement, enjoyment, compatibility, patience. Asses the ability to connect to each other.

Anxiety - Vulnerability

If this verbal challenge is overcome, the flow becomes regulated; rather than a slalom course to be navigated with rapids and flags, it may reach calmer waters to allow a hand to be held. Anxiety is left aside for now.

Intimacy

Tests must be passed, mental boundaries respected. Intimacy. The early guest to the party, the word overshadows to remain the elephant in the room whether acknowledged or not. It is the third wheel, chaperone to each message, conversation, meeting. It listens in anticipation, lurking in the fringes, waiting for its name to be spoken, alluded to.

Minefield - Fear

Intimacy has its time, even then, each touch, sigh, bodily response may signal a realisation of betrayal of another. A minefield from past to present, to be navigated with care and patience. For those seeking the restoration of past intimacies. A new person is a mind and soul alone, it cannot become unintentionally a portal to an old love.

Equally, to another, a word or tone may trigger a portcullis to descend. This is a long and tortuous path, strewn with hazards. A touch rushed, sharp word spoken, silences, scorn. Mind and body are locked as the memories of abuse or trauma revived, secure behind bars, they become a spectator and prisoner of the past once more. *Patience is the key.*

36

By Degrees

In Sydney they met, the Gas Company girl,
and the tall dark Waterford man.
She followed love the wrong way around the world.
Traded 40-degree summers for rainbows
over the Comeragh Mountains.

Set down roots in a small cottage on family land
in a climate where a few degrees separated
Summer from Winter.
Condensation painting mould on bathroom tiles.

Rabbits raided her garden, Mr Fox stole her hens.
Mr Duck became a widower, adopted by the geese
- Grace, Geraldine Gwendoline but tolerated by Gus.
Taken under their large white wings.

She raised a baby
who ran wild with Shetlands and Dartmoors
across a view wasted on ponies.
Her pride and joy,
the dark-haired boy grey tall
then moved away, education gave him wings.

No common ground,
the glue that held the pair together,
cracked and split.
He returned to the small cottage,

She uprooted to warm Andulsion hills.
Traded soft Waterford rain that painted mould
for arid summers that cracked the ground.
Separated by degrees, she began her next chapter.

The Path

A thought washed through my mind,
a clarity, a cleansing to bring peace.
At times people enter your life,
space is cleared to afford them a starring role.

This may not be how life cast their role in your life,
possibly only destined to be brief
but their contribution long lasting,
a vital part of your tapestry.

Every relationship makes its mark,
once its role is fulfilled.
They may only share a portion of your journey.
A path to be trodden together for a while.

This is does not mean
you will not travel together again,
but you must accept that
there is another path to tread just now.

The Size of Him

He rolled in after closing time, like a lord.
The house had long gone to bed.
Full of drink, he raised the wife
to cook a fry fit for a king.

An exchange of sharp words, flurry of fists.
She landed a defensive punch.
thrown from tired arms that
hand washed for his six children.

Out for the count,
dragged by the collar,
snoring to his bed.

His shiner met him in the mirror.
Examined closely as he shaved.
Darlin, you should have seen the size of him.
He told the wife over a plate of rashers
and freshly baked bread.

Paper Thin Walls

The newspapers sensationalized your story.
Jeanette B of class 5D.
I sat near you in physics,
neither of us destined for science.

We were in the same child development class,
You had a private project concealed
under your extra-large blue school jumper.
No-one guessed your secret.

You were kind, quiet, hard to know.
How did you drown out baby screams?
Through paper thin walls
of a small council flat.

Where your troubled boyfriend
heated a screwdriver on a 2-bar electric fire.
Pressed the metal hard against yielding baby flesh.
Scorched lines between old cigarette burns.

Destined to live only a few short months.
This poor baby spent less time
outside your blue school jumper
than when it was concealed safely beneath.

White Knight

Once upon a time of sorrow, I met a white knight.
In him, I endowed the role of my saviour.
A knight who could not ride a horse.

So enamored was I,
I polished armor he never wore.

Subjected my needs to his,
unasked for
although eventually expected.

Projected a hero image
onto an
unsuitable canvas.

The Visit

The day after your visit
I washed my hair to tame the frizz
and painted pink my smile.

I cut the lawn,
fixed broken things
and completed all the jobs
I wished I had done the day before
you arrived
and lifted my heart.

Pure Romance
for Jenny & Dean

Slender hand raised to salute a setting sun.
Reflections in the cool waters of Lake Garda,
the glint of diamond,
the warm glow of the band of gold.

Two hearts linked in harmony
against the Italian sunset.
An affirmation of love,
an intention of mutual happiness.

Pure romance.

Find Your Tribe

Darkness.
No sense of belonging to anything, anyone.
Begin a process of change to discover oneself.
Evolve, transform to find true self-expression.

Enter a world of possibility through an adventure.
Learn a new skill; use colour to paint your visions,
learn to play music, write.
The portal to enter a world previously unknown,
perceived to be inadmissible, in your world of limitation.

Joyous to be found worthy of inclusion,
a valuable member with worthwhile contributions.
A welcome addition to the group.

Priceless, to find your tribe, slot into your niche.
Celebrate your talent amongst those who understand.
Be careful to set aside time in this sacred space.

Fulfilment of potential.
A transformational experience to a life half lived.
Gather the courage required to undertake the journey
from darkness to live your life in the light.
To at last find your tribe.

Observations

A careless seed sown
may be plucked early.
Deemed to be a weed.

Budgerigar

Sideways profile.
Large stomach fluorescent green golf shirt,
received as a present.
One of many in the wardrobe.

Red nose from shouting, about something and nothing.
Short heavy steps taken, stomping
about to make a point.

Family nickname,
the same as my childhood pet budgie.
Always made me smile, suppress a giggle.

The name brought forth an image.
A very large, angry
green budgerigar.

A secret never shared. Till now.
Saw me through many years,
when little else raised laughter.

This image,
a lifeline,
gave me endless joy.

The Lost Baby Jesus

The baby Jesus got lost.
Unpacked with the others
then hidden away.

Waiting in the wings
for the big day,
which came and went.

In the crib,
questions abound.

The three wise men are clueless
and the shepherd looks sheepish.
Mother and Father are worried.

The bookcase
has been searched high and low
but of baby Jesus, there is no sign.

The sheep,
if they know anything
are saying nothing.

Ode to the Mop

The mop stands guard
between the patio door and the side door
in the Irish rainy season from January to December.

There may be the exception of a dry week
in April or May or possibly September
but never expect seven fair days together.

The mop remains on duty, patrols almost hourly to erase
muddy footprints or paws.
Followed from one door to the other.
Swish, swish, back and forth.

Occasionally the mop is left to stand between the doors
to lean idle in the middle.
Where my mother would have said
it is neither use nor ornament.

Milo and I

Milo stared through the gate.
Like me, he had had a haircut.
We shared a moment.
Both had lost our COVID curls.

Milo now had the smooth look of a chocolate Labrador,
only the hint of the curl at the floppy ear
betrayed the springer.

Not for him the six week appointment.
He wore his natural colour.
He was all style and he knew it.

Colours of Belonging

*Written for people like me who don't quite fit in
and don't really understand why.*

I am a stained -glass window, alight with a smile,
the illusion of wholeness.
Coloured broken shards welded together with resilience.
Blues, reds, greens and yellows of life's struggles to conform.
Fit the version of someone else's normal.

Serve endless years of school,
endure stages of teenage rebellion,
discover that music can bind
or divide in the search to find a community,
a sense of belonging.

Navigate the social jungle
with personality profiling.
Team building,
corporate personality tests.

A window to the real you.
Serve to isolate?
Confirm the reality of difference.
Celebrate the individual?

Defined in colours,
employees hide in corporate silence from angry reds,
appease blues with facts and detail.

Tread carefully around greens, to avoid offence.
Bond with other yellows, so few, so familiar, so creative.

Learn to conform, network, connect.
Add value, be more productive, be more effective.
Enhance the culture of the business family.

Prove you are worthy,
you belong.
Survive.

Eventually learn to love oneself
before the appeasement of others.

Broken shards welded together by resolve,
shone through with a smile
to light the colours of life.
The illusion of wholeness.

**First published in Undercover Wexford Magazine 2022

Bitterness

Refuse
the
gift
of
poison.

If left
untouched,
unheeded,

it remains the property of the bearer.

Journey on unburdened to peace.
Unsullied by the bitterness of another.

Wisdom

*Written for the invisible people
who are never truly valued.*

Birthdays are not about getting older.
Determine value by age.
Undermine the young, underestimate the old.

Years are about getting wiser.
Age becomes a handle to open doors to opportunity.
Or barrier to close the doors on experience.

Understand that knowledge is measured
beyond years,
beyond numbers.

Speculate accumulated wisdom.
Age does not guarantee
access to that which has no key.

Risen Shards

The heart needs
to purge old hurts
those embedded shards that detach
to pierce through the skin
as a splinter risen.

A necessary healing.
An exorcism of mind.

Anxiety

Before sleep,
wish on the full moon in eclipse
for peace of mind.
Battle recommences as eyelids close.

Anxiety waves the baton to signal the charge.
Despair invades, *Hope* and *Optimism*
gather forces, ever faithful friends.
Confidence tormented;
held captive by rampaging *Doubt.*

Forces of good
must endure at great odds
the endless siege,
during the hours of darkness.

A champion must surface to fight the foe,
strong enough to overcome the mighty forces
of *Anxiety;*
to win the battles locked deep inside the mind.
Until then, there will be no peace at night.

Illusion

When we met,
I imprinted values
I believed were shared.

Created a common bond.
Observed implied
rules of behaviour.

When the illusion shattered
Amongst the shards of our relationship.
I met the person, you never were.

Mask

Are you worn out yet?

Presenting the version
of you
under the mask
that you feel others expect.

Daughters of Eve

When will the legacy of Eve be left behind?
The temptation of an apple left rot in the ground.

When will a girl or woman be able to step outside of home,
dressed as she pleases, her choices made by the weather
and not society.

When will a walk be chosen purely for the enjoyment
of the route alone, without consideration
for time of day, darkness, isolation and her safety.

When will the blame rest on the strong shoulders
where the blame belongs, lifted from the women
who walked where they wished or dressed as they wanted?

When will this behaviour end and our paternal culture change?

The culture that excuses or defends the character of the men
who choose to attack, defile, terrorise or kill.

When will the daughters of Eve be free?

War

On the eve of yet another invasion of another country,
another war.
Images are shown of people, just like, you, me, us.
Leaving their beloved homes, family, country, life.
Leaving their young people to defend
their homeland with their lives.

Possessions crammed into backpacks, or if lucky, cars.
Streams of people flee to the thunder of bombs,
loud as the pounding of their hearts.

Possessions chosen for their worth, warmth, memories.
Discarded as they grow too heavy when fear
overcomes the need to keep them.
People like me you, us, travel to an unknown destination
with the hope of welcome.

My home is warm, peaceful, flowers bloom
awakened to Spring, the colours lift my spirits.
My grown children are safe to live their own lives.
My family near and far are safe, their troubles
the usual ones of the West.

Unless the greedy gaze of a superpower seeks
to take what we have.
Then they will wage war on the innocent.

On the eve of war, what would you take?
How much could you pack?
Where are your family, are they still safe?
Where could you go?

Will our young people have to defend our country
when life descends into chaos, cruelty,
driven by greed and the need for power.
War.

Observers

I see faces in the trees,
withdrawn to observe
how humanity defiles
the contours of the land.

The production
of excess goods
destined as landfill waste.

Consumers seek satisfaction,
pursue the allure of the purchase
endless need, unfulfilled want.

Nature, the most precious
resource of all.

Ravaged for
temporary gain
by transient souls.

Time colours our history,
remembered through
washed out shades of dove grey,
powder pink and dusty blue.

Memories

Annagassan Beach
For Mary, Debbie & Thomas

Summer 1971, my Mother brought
the blue anchor bobbins in O'Flynns of Ardee.

Wild waves of Burns hair scraped into pigtails
for the trip to Annagassan beach.

My father drove our mustard Moskavitch
packed to the gills with adults;
children perched on laps, ashtrays full,
windows down.

Recall the precisely cut vanilla icecream,
measured against the steel ruler to be carefully placed
between two wafers passed reverently to each child.

A creamy distraction to sweeten disappointment.
An invasion of brown blobs stranded on the
beach in warm sunshine.

Jellyfish as large as dinner plates,
washed up awaiting the return of the afternoon tide.

Four content cousins sitting on a seawall,
my pigtails dangling in blue anchor bobbins
over a navy and white sailor dress.
Brand new, a perfect fit.

** First published in "Around Each Bend",
a compilation of Tipperary Writers by Margaret Galvin (2021)

The Milking

In memory of my Uncles Tommy & Packie Burns

Light brown coat worn for milking
The same shade as the brown bag that held split donuts
fresh from the Ardee Bakery van.
Old suit trousers tucked into black wellies,
tweed flat cap to allow the rain to run off.

Early morning and evening,
The sound of the milking machine, deep moos of the cows.
Calves brought the spring in and the milk.
Soft brown eyes as the lorries drove them away.

Summer evenings, walking the cows to the field.
Hazel stick in hand, shirt sleeves rolled up
to windburned elbows.
Up and down the hills, arms outstretched
to hunt back the rogues.
A shout to the following children,
Stand back, stand back there now.

Black and white tails lifted,
to emit a stream of brown muck, splat
Splashed onto warm tarmac.
Mucky barefoot children tiptoe around the fresh cow pats.

Gate closed, freisian cows sway toward
the distant Mountains of Mourne,
the setting sun sinks into the peat bogs.

Stroll back to Mullenstown for the tea.
Split donuts from the van, creamy milk, frothing in the jug.
Stood to keep on the cold stone floor of the pantry.

Old Tramore
Coast Guard Station

Old Tramore Coast Guard station perched high on the hill
now serves tea and luscious cakes.
A refuge from the wind within thick stone walls,
often painted white sash windows, polished curled brass latches.

Thick bottled glass distorts walkers on the long sandy strand.
To the right, the lonely stance of the Metal Man,
sweep the gaze across the bay, white horses ride the waves.
On the left the bright lights of the funfair.

Where once this view was scoured for souls to save.
Distressed swimmers taken by an outgoing tide,
rescue weekend sailors who under-estimate the sea
or over-estimate their skill.

In service for over a century where many lives
were risked at the mercy of wild waves,
Jagged grey rocks and precarious rip tides.

Today the soft clink of china,
cup upon saucer
replaces the clank of chains
that hauled the lifeguard crew safely home.

The Scaffold

My brothers worked on the scaffold,
saw the London skyline as only the pigeons do.
Trod the narrow boards high above state institutions,
office blocks and high rises.

Walked in steel toe capped boots, grease-stained t-shirts, ripped jeans
through hallowed halls of London's palaces, museums and
endured the dirty crawl through small attic spaces onto the roofs.

Tanned and muscled from throwing the pipes, raising the loads to
the dizzy heights above the highest buildings as the sun rose.
Devoured full English breakfast in the local greasy spoon cafes
with plenty of tea, as office and shop workers filled the streets.

Before the time of safety officers, had knowledge required of the
ground, how weights were balanced on tons of aluminum by
well paid, fearless men with total disregard for their own safety.
Flying like squirrels 300ft above the ground,
no harness worn, deemed a barrier to movement and flexibility.

During storms, awoke to the shattering ring of the house phone to
attend a dangerous structure while London slept.
A given part of the job to make the building safe
balancing on slippery boards and tubes soaked to the skin,
scalded by the piercing cold in bitter high winds.

Rivalry between firms would have required the U.N. to sort.
Arguments with cabbies about lorries blocking small streets.
Move on mate, how else would the gear be raised?

At times after a hard day, a quiet pint raised to a passed friend
who always stood his round; but one day *missed* his step.

Swalecliffe Chalet c.1973

First Spring trip to the Kent coast,
packed into our mustard yellow Moskavitch
slow through heavy London traffic
until the freedom of the A2.

My heart sings across the Medway Bridge
with the glimpse of the sea.

Dance impatiently at the wooden chalet door until
the key is found at the bottom of the handbag.
Dad whistles as Mum unpacks the biscuits, puts on the kettle.

Anorak zipped tight, three gears squeak
in protest on the rusty bike.
Cycle two miles of coastal path from Swalecliffe to Herne Bay.
Race fat ponies behind bare hawthorn hedges.

Survey the trampolines covered and still, a field of canvas.
Springs will strain and creak from Easter to September
under tumbling children; 10p a go.

Peddle slowly back around the curve of the bay.
White horses crash against pebble shores,
loud the suck and draw.
High tide rages against the stepped black timber breakers.

Unwrap soggy cheese & tomato sandwich in silver foil,
spiced with pepper, harsh winds tangle knots into salty hair.
Take the kite to the flat field, iridescent plastic scales
shimmer on the emerald dragon of Wales.
Run backward fast to catch the sea breeze.
Dip and dive above the waves, crash entangled in rough grass.

Heart full, just can't wait for summer weekends.
Swim in the cold sea, float to shore on an inner tube.
Dig for lug worm at low tide for eel fishing.
Cram jam jars full of death; cruel glass coffins of Kentish crabs.

Chalet aired, parents are packed, ready for home.
The lethal finger trap of the iron
fold-out bed oiled, door locked.
Return under harsh yellow street lamps, car sick, green.

Kildemock –
the Jumping Church

The jumping church of Kildemock,
stands near Ardee, Co. Louth.
This was parish land given by St Patrick
at the dawn of Christianity to his disciple Dimock.

To enter push back the black wrought iron gate
or climb the smooth stone style.
Ancient yews stand sentry in the graveyard
of this small 12th century chapel twice witness to God's wrath.

In the corner of the graveyard, find a gravestone split in two.
It was during mass that lighting struck the fallen stone
to visit terror upon men who diced upon the names of the dead.
Stark warning to those who truant from God
to defile this holy place.

Marvel at the chapel west wall leaning at an impossible angle.
This wall jumped during the wild storm of 1715,
moved by magical powers or holy anger
at the freshly interred body of a rogue within its walls.
During the night a great storm arose
to lash the fury of the heavens
to leave this villain's body without.

Close to Kildemock is Garrets Fort.
Legend has it that in this raised mound
Gearoid Iarla and his soldiers lie asleep on horseback.
Heads fallen down over horse's manes,
hands upon their swords.

The sleeping army awaits
a six fingered man or redhaired woman
– depending upon to whom you speak.
Draw the sword from its scabbard to break the spell,
for these warriors to ride to battle again.

Kildemock chapel is lost to time,
The chancel still faces north-east to the blue Cooley hills.
A broken shell of Christianity surrounded by an old graveyard.
A thousand years later the famous west wall still stands.

71

Christmas Pudding

Mother and I travelled miles for a good Christmas jumble sale.
No greater pleasure than to snaffle a bargain.
On one such jaunt, a winter coat was procured.

In fact, a large dark green adults cape, lined with cold black
satin.
Black velvet baby doll collar,
low arm holes trimmed with black corduroy.
So heavy, it had to be worn home rather than carried.

At the bus stop, my pre-pubescent pleas fell on deaf ears.
The cape was pronounced a perfect fit; though my reflection
revealed two legs poking out of a green dome.
Topped by a bright red face under a page boy haircut.

Finally, a red London double decker bus arrived,
full of Christmas shoppers.
We squashed into the lower deck;
a seat given up for Mother.

The bus weaved through busy traffic,
my short arms stretched from under the low cape armholes
to reach the pole, the cape tipped back and forth to throttle.
The musty smell of the tweed rose
with the heat of the bodies around me. Red face turned green.

Returned finally to the safety of our kitchen,
my father took one look and quipped,
She looks like a Christmas Pudding.
The cape was placed in the wardrobe,
never to be seen again.

Nora's Mince

The rivalry between cooks over their signature dish can be fierce. To imply that another person cooks a dish better is a perilous thing.

Once a year, our family travelled from London to visit my Mother's childhood home in County Louth, Ireland.

Now, you may imagine that the request for Nora's mince would evoke a smile from my Mother of the annual summer holiday. You would be wrong.

Nora's mince was a dish to behold. Served in a stew bowl, as large as a dinner plate with an inch ledge for bread to perch on. It was a brown lake of smooth minced beef, small chopped onion, sunken rounds of carrot and at least five islands of potatoes. These were of course, not just any potatoes, they were Ardee, potatoes grown in Mullenstown soil. Light and loamy, producing the perfect floury potato. These were added strategically to each dinner. The children watching their plates like hawks to make sure nobody else received a larger spud, plates often being swopped around to gain advantage. The potatoes were demolished to reveal the submerged Chinese pattern, either blue and white or pink and white. The colours would peek through as the last spud was carefully wiped around to gather every drop of gravy. This was you see, not a dish given to becoming a left over.

When my Mother asked the question, ***what shall we have for dinner?*** Spoken in a good tempered tone often to the setting rays of a summer sun. The atmosphere could change in a flash. This sentence could quickly rain down on you the icy winds of betrayal.

Nora's Mince. A sharp bow of the head to the side to digest this comment. Followed by raised eyebrows, a lengthening of the neck and a dropping of the chin. ***Nora's Mince. What is wrong with my mince?***

Whatever you did, you never said, *I prefer it.* The result could be cold meat sandwiches for days if you were lucky.

My Mother's mince, was also a thing of beauty. But, after Nora's Mince, it was a shabby second. My Mother quite rightly said that Nora cheated by replacing the fat from the meat with the addition of Oxtail Soup and a dash or HP or YR sauce depending on the mood.

In general appearance, there was little to choose between the two dishes. For me, where my Mother went wrong, was by adding lard to fry off the fatty butchers mince. This combination left a sheen under the strip light of the kitchen. A brown lake glistening with a slight oil slick, served with crusty white cob bread and potatoes, and butter My parents loved this, *It will put meat on your Bones.* They said. As if, with an Irish Mother who bestowed so many spuds on each dinner, they dwarfed the plate, I needed more meat on my bones. I hate fat. The residue makes me shudder and I am no vegetarian.

My parents could discuss the merits of potatoes like others talked of wine. My mother was a great cook and my father a gardener who could grow almost anything. Home grown vegetables and their merits would be discussed at great lengths, a discussion of experts, on trend before their time as it now seems. However, Dad's great disappointment was carrots, they could not be grown due to the 10 mature trees at the boundary of the garden, Horse Chestnuts, Beech and doomed Elms.

Concealed under a shepherd's pie, Mum's mince was King. The oil was absorbed into the potato topping, to become crispy golden brown peaks. King Edwards, whilst not as fluffy or flavoured as Mullenstown potatoes, could hold their own mashed in a shepherd's pie. Towering above the carrots, onions, mushrooms, this mash was a veritable crust of happiness. Wonderful on the day or comfortingly covered in rich brown thick gravy part mince juice and Bisto for tea the next day. Adoration of this dish was however, no consolation for the words, *I'd like Nora's Mince for dinner please.*

Red Car - Revenge

I left school in the early 1980s, that first summer I began work as a lowly solicitor's clerk. I photocopied, collected documents from Government institutions for property searches, delivered court documents to barristers' quarters in beautiful buildings such as the Inner Temple, Lincolns Inn, Old Bailey and the Royal Courts of Justice. I saw the inside of buildings that usually only a select few see. Of course, for them, not under the best of circumstances. During this time, I couldn't believe that I was paid to travel on trains around London, where I could daydream away the journey knowing that this was a job and I wasn't just skipping school.

One day, an older lady arrived for her appointment dressed to the nines to make her will. As a clerk it was my job to photocopy these documents, so I got to see the contents of her will. The fact I remember it so clearly all these years later is testimony to how funny I found it and I hope you will too.

The lady in question had been a career girl, which during her time would have been tough as she chose to not to get married but to be successful. She was a spiritly woman even though she was in her 90s. She would have lived through two world wars and the deprivations of those times. She swopped stories while she waited with our lively receptionist who always dressed in leather trousers, they were kindred spirits. Our lady had been a wild girl, she owned a red sports car which had seen some action and hair-raising times.

This red car was clearly coveted by her nephew, John who was in his mid-fifties and having what she described as a "mid-life crisis". He wished to re-invent himself and the car was part of that image. It was a collector's item worth some money but more, it was a status symbol of the person he wished to be.

The long and the short of it was that he visited often because he wanted the car. The conversations always were around the car, how it was rusting and under-used in her garage. It seemed to break his heart at its abandonment. He was a greedy man who was not visiting his aunt to keep her company, get her shopping or do those little jobs that a stronger person could do. He was not there to brighten her day, he wanted that car. Finally, she must have succumbed during one of these visits; she came up with a plan, the will. I will share with you that the will said he would indeed get the car.

In time the lady passed. The nephew attended the office for the will to be read. He was handed the keys, the car was to be delivered to his home. He was a little puzzled but commented that perhaps there were mechanical issues after not being used for so long. Leaving the office, the nephew was as happy as a lark because he finally got what he wanted. The solicitor smiled as he showed him out.

I can only imagine John's surprise at the car that was delivered to his door.

A three-foot red metal box unloaded from a breakers yard lorry; which indeed now did have mechanical issues. On that box tied with a red bow was a wee letter from his aunt. Her final words.

> *Dear John,*
>
> *It is with joy that I give you the car that you have always coveted.*
> *Much love   Auntie xxx*

Her last act, the will, her sweetest revenge.

Christchurch Road

I grew up in Christchurch Road, London. I am the youngest of our family, my two older brothers were late teens when I was born. Mum was 47 with one ovary. Her boys reared, I am sure she thought she could relax. She should have listened to the fortune teller on Brighton Pier, who had foretold 17 years before, that "She would have a girl when she least expected it.

My house was always filled with people, never lonely. A four storey Victorian house with four generations living in it most of the time. If things went wrong, they always said "as long as you tried, your best", or "if it's meant to be, it will happen".

We recycled everything, before it was fashionable, broken washing machines as cat beds, Dad had two televisions side by side, one for picture, one for sound, kept because they both worked. My house was full of books on every subject. It was magical, so many places to hide.

The entrance hall was wide, the door to the Basement flat was always open, steep stairs meant everyone developed a special knock followed by HELLO to avoid popping down if no-one answered. The hall was the place where you understood the house. It caught all the smells of cooking, various sounds from four flats. Different radio stations, Mum in the Basement listening to Radio 4 with Just a Minute; Kenneth Williams distinctive nasal voices; Radio 1, from the two middle flats and gunshots from a Western film from Mrs Rowe's attic flat.

Each flat had beautiful plaster ceiling mouldings, marble fireplaces. At eighteen, I took my own flat and collapsed my first ceiling. I put the washing machine on then went out.

A cloth from the draining board fell into the sink during the final spin, dirty water emptied into the sink, spilled to the floor, seeped slowly for hours, water running down the central light fitting below until finally collapsing the ceiling with a roar of heavy plaster about my spritely 97 year old grandmother who had no ceiling or electric for several days. Just one of her narrow escapes, having lived through two world wars, she just got on with it though, no moaning or drama.

My flat above Grandma's had views into the horse chestnut trees and beech trees. These flats had the best washing lines in the street, stretching from the kitchen windows 100 yards away, high into the trees fitted by my scaffolding brothers. Hanging out washing was an art form. Open the sash window, balance it so that it didn't decapitate you, lean out as far as you dared, pegs in one hand, wet clothes in the other. Don't drop anything or hang too much in case the line snapped. Get the weight right. One or two loads, but not too many towels, pulling the washing rope in and out in good or bad weather, hauling like a navvy facing down over a 40ft drop.

Having a bath was not for the faint hearted either. You needed a certain level of dexterity. Three flats shared the bathroom, a small L-shaped room with a high ceiling that faced the busy road. A freezing ceramic cast iron bathtub presided over the room directly under the tall windowsill. High above this, perched a temperamental Aston gas boiler fed by 50p coins from a meter. Running a good bath was a skill and required the precision of a safe cracker. Turn the knob for a thin stream of barely warm water which dropped 3 ft below, 20 minutes yielded 4 inches of water.

Turning the knob too fast would give cold water, too slow meant the gas went out. Relighting the gas was tricky, it could ignite with a loud bang, causing loudly muttered curses, clasping of hearts. It was always safer to put 50p in the meter, just in case some other beggar had used your credit. If this ran out, the Aston would speed up and spew out freezing cold water. It was a sensitive beast to be soothed, approached with caution. It terrified me.

To get in the bath, you needed to be a contortionist. You couldn't dress the lower frosted window so there was no protection for your modesty from the queue of traffic below when getting in or out of the bath. It was best to bend low near the door, crouching walk to the bath, turn sideways, flip into the bath avoiding the cold ceramic rim. Spin quickly, whilst sloshing the water up and down the sides to get warm, sitting back even though your shoulders were twitching from the cold bath walls.

The small square unglazed window near the door handle could allow a hand flip the lock incase a child got locked in. Once in the bath, the sound of footsteps on the landing made you wonder if you had locked the door, relaxation ended.

No wonder, I prefer a shower.

***First published in Kilkenny City Local Radio,
in the awarded series - Women's Bits, a memoir series of podcasts.*

The Guide

Here is a guide to navigate my world.
There is little balance here, I am all or nothing.
I either like you or I don't, I am not for half measures.

I value honesty, don't bother lying, I will know.
Something said or unsaid will blip on my radar.
Say what you have to say but don't shout.

Be genuine, I may not like it
but then truth may sometimes hurt.
Don't let me imagine, those are shark infested waters.

I wear my heart on my sleeve, I am a good friend
But I can't be bothered with enemies.
Good luck and goodbye.

My attention span is short and intense,
probably best to tell me while I am walking.
No need for small words; words are my world; their nuances
and meanings are my puzzles.

My books, music and writing are as precious to me
as my children and animals.
Beware, my Mother said I slept in the knife drawer,
sharp as a tack.

So welcome to my world,
be kind or be gone.

About the Author

Theresa B. Jones is originally from London, England.
She has two wonderful children.
Lives near the beautiful Comeragh Mountains, Ireland.

Spends most of the week working at as a Doc Specialist,
the rest walking her dog, hacking out on Buster and writing.

She writes narrative poetry which tell short stories in a few verses.
She is part of a wonderful collective of writers, takes part in Spoken
Word events in local festivals such as Clonmel Junction Festival,
Applefest; and the Clancy Festival with writers of Poetry Plus
through Margaret O'Brien and Linda Fahey of Tudor Artisan Hub -
who make possible exciting collaborations with writers, artists and
musicians on projects. These festivals and events are opportunities
that she never imagined would be available to a South London girl.

First collection published: **Servant of Time, Poetry Collection.**
Servant of Time: Poetry Collection by Theresa Jones | Goodreads
https://www.goodreads.com/book/show/56039248-servant-of-time

**If you enjoyed this poetry collection,
please review me on Goodreads**
Waterfall of Intentions: Poetry Collection by Theresa Jones –

Printed in Great Britain
by Amazon

78548338R00047